THE SUPER BOWL

CHASING FOOTBALL IMMORTALITY

MATT DOEDEN

MILLBROOK PRESS · MINNEAPOLIS

Millbrook Press
A division of Lerner Publishing Group, Inc.
241 First Avenue North
Minneapolis, MN 55401 USA

For reading levels and more information, look up this title at www.lernerbooks.com.

Main body text set in Adobe Garamond Pro Regular 14/19.
Typeface provided by Adobe Systems.

Library of Congress Cataloging-in-Publication Data

Names: Doeden, Matt, author.
Title: The Super Bowl : chasing football immortality / Matt Doeden.
Description: Minneapolis : Lerner Publications, [2017] | Series: Spectacular sports |
  Includes bibliographical references and index.
Identifiers: LCCN 2016042224 (print) | LCCN 2017006836 (ebook) | ISBN
  9781512427547 (lb : alk. paper) | ISBN 9781512451153 (eb pdf)
Subjects: LCSH: Super Bowl—History—Juvenile literature. | Football—History—
  Juvenile literature.
Classification: LCC GV956.2.S8 D63 2017 (print) | LCC GV956.2.S8 (ebook) |
  DDC 796.332/648—dc23

LC record available at https://lccn.loc.gov/2016042224

Manufactured in the United States of America
1-41487-23350-2/17/2017

CONTENTS

INTRODUCTION
THE BIG GAME

The quarterback takes the snap and drops back to pass. Flashes light up the stands as the fans snap photos. The sound of cheering is almost deafening. The clock ticks down—5 . . . 4 . . . 3 . . . Defenders crash through the line and converge on the quarterback. He spins out of a tackle, turns, and heaves the ball toward the end zone.

More than 100 million people watch on TV as the ball sails through the air. Everything rides on one play. An entire National Football League (NFL) season comes down to this: the Super Bowl.

It's the biggest game of the pro football season and arguably the biggest sporting event of the year. Since its modest beginnings in the late 1960s, the Super Bowl has become something larger than a championship game. It has become a cultural institution, an unofficial national holiday, and a game that unites fans and nonfans alike. And it all started with one simple question: Which football team is the best in the world?

Facing page: Jets fly over Levi's Stadium in Santa Clara, California, before the start of Super Bowl 50 on February 7, 2016.

Pro football in the 1920s didn't look much like the modern game.

1 FROM CHAOS TO CHAMPIONSHIPS:
THE MAKING OF THE BIG GAME

Representatives of 11 pro football teams gathered at an automobile showroom on a hot, humid day in 1920. It hardly seemed like the start of something big. The loosely organized meeting in Canton, Ohio, didn't even have enough chairs for all the people present. Some had to sit on the showroom's cars.

Football as a professional sport was in its infancy. College football was developing a loyal following, but the pro game remained largely an afterthought with fans. Teams were scattered throughout the nation, mainly in the Midwest. They had no central organization. They didn't even share a common set of official rules. The part-time players went to the highest bidder, bouncing from team to team, and even the teams with winning records—including the Canton Bulldogs, the reigning champions—were losing money.

Pro football was on the brink of collapse. If it was to survive, something had to change. And Ralph Hay, the owner of the Bulldogs, had a plan. He had already approached three fellow team owners about banding together to start the American Professional Football Conference (APFC). It was time to see if other owners were ready to buy into the idea. Hay made his case before the men gathered in the showroom. In the new league he envisioned, teams would share a common rule book, they would not raid one another's rosters, and the size of contracts would be limited.

For two hours, the men hammered out an outline for the league. Hay's vision became reality. The APFC—still disjointed, disorganized, and largely dysfunctional—changed its name to the American Professional Football Association (APFA) and began its first season just a few weeks later. Despite its shortcomings, the APFA marked the jumping-off point for organized professional football. Less than two years later, the league changed its name to the National Football League.

THE DAWN OF THE NFL CHAMPIONSHIP

For more than a decade, the NFL remained a very loosely organized league. Franchises came and went. Teams picked which teams they wanted to play, including non-NFL teams, and scheduled games however they wanted to. They didn't even play the same number of games. The NFL had no playoffs, so champions were determined by the regular-season winning percentages.

Chaos was the way of the young league, and that was never truer than in the 1932 season. The Green Bay Packers led the NFL with 10 victories. Yet at the time, the league discarded all ties when calculating winning percentages. And based on winning percentages, the Packers' 10–3–1 mark left them behind both the Chicago Bears (6–1–6) and the Portsmouth Spartans (6–1–4). After throwing out the tie games, the Bears and Spartans were both left with 6–1 records.

CHARTER MEMBERS

Only two of the original APFA teams remain in the NFL today. The Decatur Staleys moved to Chicago in 1921 and won the APFA title that year. In 1922 the team changed its name to the Chicago Bears *(below, in 1925)*.

The other APFA charter member was also Chicago-based. The Chicago Cardinals remained in the Windy City until 1960, when the team moved to St. Louis. The Cardinals were on the move again in 1988, becoming the Phoenix Cardinals. In 1994 they changed their name to the Arizona Cardinals.

Both teams thrived in the early NFL, winning multiple titles. But they haven't had as much success in the modern era. The Bears have won one Super Bowl, and the Cardinals haven't won any.

This tie would change the NFL forever, but only because of highly unusual circumstances that followed. The NFL had a tiebreaker in place—the two teams' head-to-head record in the regular season. But while the Bears and Spartans had met twice in the regular season, both games had resulted in ties. The NFL had no rule to resolve the deadlock. The idea of a split title wasn't appealing to anyone— the league included. So the stage was set for a first in pro football: a winner-take-all championship game.

In what was already a unique situation, things got still stranger. The teams were set to meet at Chicago's Wrigley Field on December 18. But blizzards swept through the region, and experts predicted bitterly cold temperatures that could endanger players and fans. So the game was moved indoors, to Chicago Stadium.

Fans could get close to the action at Chicago Stadium for the 1932 NFL Championship.

The stadium, however, wasn't big enough to house a full-sized football field. So the 1932 NFL Championship was played on a field that measured just 80 yards from goal line to goal line and was also 10 yards narrower than a field should be! If that wasn't bad enough, the loose-dirt field offered little footing and hadn't been properly cleaned after a circus had been in town a week before.

The game itself was a flop, beginning with the temperature outdoors being well above zero, far warmer than predicted. Inside, on a surface and field unfit for football, neither team could generate much offense. Finally, in the fourth quarter, Chicago fullback Bronko Nagurski

Bronko Nagurski stretches out his throwing arm during practice before the 1932 NFL Championship. Nagurski's pass to Red Grange was the game's only touchdown.

threw a touchdown pass to Red Grange. The Bears went on to a 9–0 victory.

Even though that 1932 title game was a disaster, it inspired a major change in the NFL. In 1933 the league split its teams into two divisions. The Bears won the Western Division, while the New York Giants claimed the Eastern Division. The teams met for the first official NFL Championship. This time, the game lived up to its billing. It was, at that time, an offensive shootout. The Giants led, 21–16, in the final minutes. That's when the Bears' Nagurski threw a 14-yard pass to Bill Hewitt, who then tossed it to Billy Karr. Karr streaked into the end zone for the winning touchdown.

The days of crowning a champion based solely on the regular season were gone for good.

THE CHAMPIONSHIP YEARS

For more than three decades, the NFL Championship was the jewel of the pro football season. Over that time, some of the league's most memorable games were played for the sport's top prize. Among them was the 1934 title game, which saw a rematch between the Bears and Giants, this time in New York.

The undefeated Bears were heavy favorites. The night before the game, a storm dumped freezing rain onto New York's Polo Grounds. The field was hard and slick. Players on both teams slipped and slid as their cleats provided almost no

New York Giants defenders *(white headgear)* swarm Chicago's Bronko Nagurski *(right)* at the Polo Grounds in 1934.

solid footing. The Bears controlled what little action there was, however, pulling out to a 10–3 halftime lead.

During the first half, Giants end Ray Flaherty had suggested to head coach Steve Owen that rubber-soled sneakers might offer better grip. So Owen sent an equipment manager to nearby Manhattan College. There—with the school's blessing—the equipment manager emptied the lockers of the school's basketball team. In the second half, the Giants came out with the borrowed shoes. The new footwear made all the difference. The Giants ran circles around the Bears, who were still slipping and sliding in their useless cleats. New York outscored Chicago 27–3 in the second half to end the Bears' bid for a perfect season.

In 1940 the Bears faced the Washington Redskins in the title game. Washington had beaten Chicago just three weeks earlier. But this rematch belonged to the Bears. Quarterback Sid Luckman led the team up and down the field, while Washington appeared helpless to stop them. When it was over, Chicago was celebrating a 73–0 victory. It remains the largest margin of victory in NFL history—including the regular season.

The 1950 NFL Championship introduced a new power to the league. The Cleveland Browns had ruled the short-lived All-America Football Conference (AAFC), and they joined the NFL when the AAFC dissolved. In their first NFL season, the Browns went 10–2 behind the play of star quarterback Otto Graham. They faced the Los Angeles Rams for the title. The Browns' amazing run appeared to be over as they trailed the Rams, 28–20, entering the fourth quarter. But Cleveland stormed back for a 30–28 victory. It was the start of six straight NFL Championship game appearances for the Browns. They won again in two of those games, in 1954 and 1955.

The 1958 championship game between the Baltimore Colts and the Giants earned the nickname the Greatest Game Ever Played. Johnny Unitas, the Colts

Johnny Unitas (19) heaves the ball down the field during the 1958 title game. Unitas played for 17 seasons with the Colts and one season with the San Diego Chargers before retiring in 1973.

25-year-old quarterback, led a furious last-second drive to tie the game at the end of the fourth quarter. That set up something that had never before happened in an NFL game—overtime. It was sudden death for the championship. The Giants won the coin toss, but the Colts forced them to punt. Unitas took over. He led an 80-yard drive that ended in a game-winning touchdown run from fullback Alan Ameche. The excitement, which was broadcast on national television, helped fuel an explosion of interest in the NFL.

A CHALLENGER EMERGES: THE AMERICAN FOOTBALL LEAGUE

The NFL had started out as a loose group of teams concentrated in the Midwest. By the end of the 1950s, it had spread across the country. It had grown from a last-ditch attempt to save a failing business into a favorite for sports fans—and a cash cow for team owners. Many wealthy businesspeople wanted to be owners, but the NFL turned most away rather than expand the size of the league.

In 1960 a group of these would-be owners banded together to form their own league. The American Football League (AFL) would compete directly with the NFL—news that was not at all welcomed by NFL owners. A bitter dispute emerged between the two leagues, with each trying to sign the best players. The AFL came out swinging. In 1960 AFL teams poached three-quarters of the players drafted in the NFL's first round by offering them more money. The bidding war between the leagues was great for the players. Salaries skyrocketed. NFL teams, stripped of their monopoly on pro football, suddenly had to pay their players market value or risk losing them to the AFL.

Previous attempts to compete with the NFL had failed. But the AFL owners came with deep pockets, as well as a broadcast deal with the ABC television network. After poor attendance in its first few seasons, the league slowly built a fan base. The 1962 AFL Championship helped boost fan interest further. The game was an all-Texas affair. The Dallas Texans jumped out to a 17–0 lead at halftime. But the two-time defending champion Houston

AFL team owners in 1960

Billy Cannon of the Oilers looks for open space to run the ball against the Texans.

Oilers fought back, scoring 17 straight points to tie the game. After almost 18 minutes of overtime, the Texans booted a game-winning field goal.

Interest in football was on the rise. Yet in the end, the AFL was not built to last. It was clear that the league would never eclipse the success and the following that the NFL had built over decades. Meanwhile, NFL owners grew increasingly frustrated over losing players to the AFL and watching their profits shrink. In 1966 the feuding leagues set aside their differences, agreeing to merge. They would operate as separate leagues until 1970, but the two league champions would meet in a new title game, the AFL-NFL World Championship Game, beginning in 1967.

THE SUPER BOWL IS BORN

The first AFL-NFL World Championship Game—later dubbed Super Bowl I—featured the NFL's Green Bay Packers and the AFL champs, the Kansas City Chiefs. The game was nothing like the spectacle fans know today, yet it drew nearly 62,000 people to the Los Angeles Memorial Coliseum in 1967.

Play in the NFL was still widely regarded as superior to that in the AFL, yet the

Elijah Pitts of the Green Bay Packers steamrollers through the Kansas City defense during Super Bowl I.

Chiefs held their own early on, trailing just 14–10 at halftime. The talent gap was real, however, as the Packers demonstrated in the second half. Quarterback Bart Starr led Green Bay to three second-half touchdowns, and the Packers walked off with a 35–10 victory.

The Packers rolled again in Super Bowl II, crushing the Oakland Raiders, 33–14. The AFL appeared unequipped to tangle with the more talented NFL. So the NFL champion Baltimore Colts seemed like a shoo-in to win Super Bowl III after the 1968 season. But the Jets stunned the football world, making good on a brash pregame victory guarantee by quarterback Joe Namath. Their 16–7 dismantling of the Colts changed the balance of power between the two leagues. By the time the leagues officially merged in 1970—becoming two conferences of the NFL, the National Football Conference (NFC) and the American Football Conference (AFC)—the playing field was level.

WHAT'S IN A NAME?

NFL and AFL teams initially agreed on the name for their title game—the AFL-NFL World Championship. Yet when Kansas City Chiefs owner Lamar Hunt casually referred to it as a Super Bowl, the name stuck. Legend says that Hunt's children had been playing with a toy called a Super Ball, leading Hunt to blurt out the iconic name.

The first two Super Bowls didn't bear the name officially, though that's how modern fans and football historians refer to them. The name finally became official for Super Bowl III, after the 1968 season. Since then Super Bowls have been identified with roman numerals. The lone exception was Super Bowl 50 in 2016.

THE GROWTH OF THE SUPER BOWL

Even in the early 1970s, the Super Bowl was popular with sports fans. But it wasn't until the end of the decade that it really started to explode. The biggest reason may have had nothing to do with the game itself but rather with the way it was covered on television. Advances in technology allowed for better coverage of the action, as well as more thorough commentary from the game's broadcast teams. Starting in 1978, the NFL experimented with airing the game in prime time when more people were watching television, rather than in the afternoon. The broadcast time helped to spike ratings, yet for some reason wasn't adopted for every Super Bowl until 1991.

By the 1990s, the Super Bowl had begun to take on its modern shape as a cultural phenomenon. The viewing experience had grown beyond the game itself. When pop legend Michael Jackson took the halftime stage in 1993, he electrified fans at home and in the stands with an energetic, dance-filled performance of hit after hit. Just like that, the halftime show became a central focus of the game, helping to ignite the interest of both football fans and people who barely cared which team won. As viewership continued to rise, advertising revenue skyrocketed. Companies filmed expensive and elaborate ads to grab public attention. For casual fans, at least, TV commercials became just as entertaining as the game itself.

Michael Jackson's performance at the Super Bowl Halftime Show in 1993 wowed both sports fans and music fans. Incredible moments like this helped make the Super Bowl the most popular sporting event in the United States.

Meanwhile, the NFL was changing the route that teams took to reach the Super Bowl. At first, the playoffs consisted of just three games: the NFL and AFL Championship games and the Super Bowl. It didn't take the league long to discover that playoff games made a lot of money. With the 1970 merger, the league split the AFC and the NFC into three divisions each. The division champions, along with a wild card in each conference, faced off for the right to represent their conference in the Super Bowl.

After the 1978 season, a second wild card team was added to each conference, bringing the total number of playoff teams to 10. In 1990 the playoff field again expanded to the modern total of 12.

By the 2000s, the Super Bowl and the spectacle that surrounds it had become an international affair, despite lukewarm interest in American football outside of North America. Media from around the world flocked to the game to cover the action on and off the field. All around the United States, people gathered at parties to enjoy the action together. Super Bowl Sunday had become an unofficial national holiday.

2 FROM HEROICS TO HEARTACHE:
HISTORY'S GREATEST SUPER BOWLS

The Super Bowl has been the highlight of the NFL season for more than half a century. Fans have seen their share of tight games and amazing finishes—as well as more than a few snoozers. What makes a Super Bowl great? It might be the stars that come out with their greatest individual efforts. It could be a heated battle between two teams fighting back and forth down to the final moments. These are the Super Bowls that have fans on the edges of their seats, both in the stadium and at home in front of their televisions. They're the games that keep fans talking for weeks, years, and even decades.

THE AFL ARRIVES
SUPER BOWL III, JANUARY 12, 1969

The first two Super Bowls provided little in the way of drama. The more established NFL dominated the AFL. By the 1968 season, many fans and reporters considered the NFL Championship to be pro football's *real* title game, with the Super Bowl being little more than a victory lap for the NFL champions, the Baltimore Colts. All that remained was the small task of dispatching the AFL champion New York Jets.

Newspapers listed Baltimore as an overwhelming 18-point favorite. But that didn't stop New York's brash young quarterback, Joe Namath, from speaking his mind. Three days before the game, Namath boldly proclaimed, "We're gonna win the game. I guarantee it."

Even under normal circumstances, Namath's guarantee seemed outlandish. Making it more so was that Don Maynard—New York's top receiver and possibly its best player—was hobbled with a hamstring injury. Yet the Jets had one thing going for them. With Maynard still in the game, the Colts were unaware of the severity of his injury. Baltimore devoted extra attention on defense to Maynard, who didn't catch a single pass in the game. Instead, he served as an effective decoy, opening up single coverage on the team's other receivers. In the second quarter, Namath led the team on an 80-yard march, capped off with a touchdown by running back Matt Snell. The 7–0 lead marked the first time an AFL team had ever led at any point in a Super Bowl.

Namath made the guarantee, but it was New York's defense that really stepped up to deliver. The Jets smothered the Colts offense, forcing five Baltimore turnovers in the game. Fans looked on in disbelief as the Jets added

"Broadway" Joe Namath's big personality and strong arm thrilled Jets fans.

three field goals to build a 16-point lead. The Colts finally broke through with a touchdown in the closing minutes, but by then, the game was out of reach. The Jets' stunning 16–7 victory stands as one of the greatest upsets in NFL history, and it served notice that the AFL was finally ready to compete with—and beat— the big, bad NFL.

POWERHOUSES COLLIDE
SUPER BOWL XIII, JANUARY 21, 1979

Many of the Super Bowls of the 1970s were one-sided affairs, lacking excitement and signature moments. One of the few bright spots of the decade was Super Bowl X, when the Pittsburgh Steelers beat the Dallas Cowboys in a tight game, 21–17. The rematch three seasons later was even better. In 1979 the two storied franchises put on a show filled with hard-hitting defense, spectacular performances, and all the drama that had been missing for most of a decade.

Pittsburgh, on the strength of quarterback Terry Bradshaw's arm, carried a 21–14 lead into the second half. In the third quarter, Dallas was driving deep into Steelers territory. The Cowboys faced third down and three to go from the Pittsburgh 10-yard line. They decided it was time for some trickery. They put 38-year-old tight end Jackie Smith into the game. Smith was on the tail end of a fine career, but he was no longer much of a pass-catching threat. Dallas was counting on the Steelers not to pay much attention to him. And it worked. The Cowboys ran a play-action pass. Dallas quarterback Roger Staubach took the snap and faked a handoff to the running back. Pittsburgh's defense took the bait, shifting toward the running back. That left Smith all alone. He ran into the end zone, completely uncovered.

Staubach saw his man and prepared to toss the easy touchdown pass. But seeing Smith all alone in the end zone rattled the quarterback. "The play was wide open,

Dallas tight end Jackie Smith falls to the ground after failing to reel in a wide-open pass from Roger Staubach.

so I tried to take a little off the ball, and I think I threw it too low," Staubach said. Smith tried to adjust to the low, yet still catchable, pass. But as he did, his feet got tangled, and he dropped the ball. A photograph of him lying on the field in anguish after the incomplete pass remains one of the Super Bowl's most tragic images. Dallas was forced to settle for a field goal to make the score 21–17.

The drama continued. Pittsburgh scored again, aided by a disputed defensive pass interference call by the referees. Things only got worse for Dallas on the kickoff that followed. Randy White fielded the kick. Pittsburgh defensive back Tony Dungy blasted into White, forcing a fumble that the Steelers recovered. The Pittsburgh offense wasted no time. One play later, Bradshaw fired an 18-yard touchdown pass to receiver Lynn Swann. The Steelers led by 18 points with less than seven minutes to play.

The Cowboys staged a desperate comeback attempt. After a drive that used up more than four minutes of the game clock, Staubach hit Billy Joe DuPree with a touchdown pass. Dallas attempted an onside kick, which Dungy was unable to field cleanly. The Cowboys recovered the ball and then scored again. Just like that, the lead was down to four points.

Dallas had one last shot. But this time, Pittsburgh secured the onside kick. The Steelers ran out the clock and became the first three-time Super Bowl champions.

JOE COOL COMES UP CLUTCH
SUPER BOWL XXIII, JANUARY 22, 1989

No team represented winning in the 1980s more than the San Francisco 49ers. The 49ers used a stout defense and the high-scoring West Coast offense to dominate the decade. It all hinged on the right arm of quarterback Joe Montana.

Yet in Super Bowl XXIII, the Cincinnati Bengals defense stifled Montana and the 49ers. Through three quarters, San Francisco was limited to a pair of field goals. The Bengals, meanwhile, pulled off an electric 93-yard kickoff return from Stanford Jennings to take a 13–6 lead into the fourth quarter.

Joe Montana (center, top) zips the ball to John Taylor. Montana was named Super Bowl Most Valuable Player (MVP) in 1981, 1984, and 1989.

But Montana's nickname, Joe Cool, hadn't come by accident. He was at his best when the lights shined brightest. Montana led a quick-hitting, four-play touchdown drive to tie the game early in the fourth quarter. Both offenses stalled before Cincinnati reclaimed the lead with a long field goal drive. As the ball sailed through the goalposts, the game clock showed 3:20 remaining.

Montana and the 49ers had one shot. The quarterback knew that the Bengals would expect him to throw passes near the sidelines. That would allow receivers to step out of bounds, stopping the clock and conserving time. He was right. Cincinnati focused their defense on the outside routes, and the middle of the field was left open. Montana took advantage. The living legend was at his best, marching his team down on a hurried, yet controlled, 11-play drive. The highlight came on a second-down play after a 49ers penalty pushed the team back 10 yards. Montana zipped a pass to Jerry Rice, who slipped past defenders and darted to the 18-yard line.

The 49ers were down by three and in field goal range, but they weren't looking to tie the game. Montana hit running back Roger Craig for 8 yards. Then, with just 39 seconds to go, Montana stepped back to throw again. At first, it looked like a broken play. Craig was Montana's primary target, but the running back had lined up in the wrong place. Meanwhile, Rice—Montana's usual go-to receiver—was covered. Calm and collected, Montana scanned the field and spotted John Taylor in the back of the end zone. He threw a strike for the game-winning touchdown. Years later, ESPN ranked it as the greatest moment in Super Bowl history. It was San Francisco's third Super Bowl title of the decade, cementing their place among the league's great dynasties.

"Joe Montana is not human," said dejected Cincinnati wide receiver Cris Collinsworth. "Every single time . . . people are counting him out, he's come back. He's maybe the greatest player who's ever played the game."

ONE YARD SHORT

SUPER BOWL XXXIV, JANUARY 30, 2000

Super Bowl XXXIV was a classic clash of styles. The St. Louis Rams relied on a quick-hitting, pass-happy offense nicknamed the Greatest Show on Turf. Quarterback Kurt Warner had entered the season as a backup of unknown talent but had ended it as the league's MVP. He relied on pinpoint timing and accuracy, hitting his speedy receivers in stride to gain yardage at a dizzying pace. The Rams' opponent was the Tennessee Titans, a team built to run with a ground-and-pound offense led by bruising running back Eddie George and quarterback Steve McNair.

The Rams had been all but unstoppable that season, and they came into the game as heavy favorites. Throughout the first half, it appeared St. Louis was on its way to another blowout, building a 16–0 lead.

In the second half, the Titans chipped away. George crashed through the St. Louis defense for a pair of touchdowns, cutting the deficit to 16–13. Meanwhile, the Titans defense did what few teams had done all season—they shut down the Rams' attack. With just 2:12 to play in the game, Tennessee kicker Al Del Greco booted a 43-yard field goal to tie it.

The Rams took over at their own 27-yard line. On the first play of the drive, Warner dropped back. Wide receiver Isaac Bruce darted down the right side of the field. Even though Bruce appeared well covered, Warner rifled a long rainbow pass to him. The ball was thrown slightly short, but Bruce adjusted, coming back to make the catch. He then sidestepped a defender and kept running. The crowd went wild as Bruce streaked in for a shocking 73-yard touchdown pass.

With less than two minutes to play and the ball at their own 12-yard line, the Titans trailed, 23–16. They needed a touchdown. The Rams fell back to deny the Titans any long passing plays, so McNair worked the short game, advancing the Titans down the field bit by bit as the clock ticked away. With 22 seconds left, McNair dropped back to pass. He was hit by two St. Louis defenders, yet somehow he lofted a 16-yard completion to receiver Kevin Dyson, who was tackled at the Rams' 10-yard line. The Titans called their final time out with five seconds remaining.

It all came down to one play. McNair dropped back and fired a quick pass to Dyson, who caught it just inside the 5-yard line. Dyson turned and charged toward the end zone. He lunged toward the goal line as defender Mike Jones grabbed him by the legs. Dyson stretched as far as he could, desperate to break the plane of the goal line with the ball, but he couldn't shake Jones. Dyson fell to the turf a single yard short of the goal line, and the final seconds passed.

The Titans had needed 88 yards, but they managed just 87 thanks to Jones' tackle. The Rams stormed the field to celebrate. ESPN later ranked the tackle as the second-greatest play in Super Bowl history.

Kevin Dyson gives everything he has, but his shoulder touches the field before he can reach the end zone.

PERFECTION?

SUPER BOWL XLII, FEBRUARY 3, 2008

The story entering Super Bowl XLII was simple. The New England Patriots had played 16 regular-season games and won all of them. Factor in two playoff wins, and it added up to 18–0. Only one team in NFL history—the 1972 Miami Dolphins—had ever achieved perfection: a perfect regular season and a Super Bowl win. With quarterback Tom Brady, receiver Randy Moss, and a drive-stopping defense, the Patriots appeared poised to join the Dolphins—newspapers listed New England as 14-point favorites. For many, the overachieving New York Giants were little more than an afterthought. Super Bowl XLII was to be New England's coronation as one of the greatest teams in NFL history.

The Giants saw it differently. They fielded the opening kickoff and marched down the field in a marathon drive that lasted nine minutes, 59 seconds, ending in a field goal. It took more time off the game clock than any drive in Super Bowl history and served notice that the Giants weren't rolling over. New York used an aggressive pass rush and an offense focused on keeping the ball to force a low-scoring, defensive contest. The Patriots, with the NFL record for points during the regular season, clung to a 7–3 lead entering the fourth quarter.

Tom Brady *(right)* and the New England offense found it tough to make headway against the New York defense during Super Bowl XLII. He was sacked five times in the game.

Then came a fourth quarter that left fans breathless. New York quarterback Eli Manning zipped a touchdown pass to rarely used receiver David Tyree. Brady and the Pats responded. With just 2:42 remaining in the game, Brady and Moss connected for a touchdown. New England led, 14–10.

Manning and the Giants took over and began a drive for the ages. The Giants scrambled to convert an early fourth down just to keep the ball. But the key play of the drive came on third down and five near midfield. Manning dropped back to throw, but the New England pass rush came on strong. Somehow, Manning managed to sidestep what appeared to be a sure sack. He whirled and launched the ball down the field. Tyree leaped over his defender, snagging the high pass and pinning it against the top of his helmet as he hit the ground. The unlikely and amazing catch went for 32 yards.

Manning didn't let his foot off the gas. A few plays later, he connected with receiver Plaxico Burress in the end zone to take the lead. The Patriots got the ball back with just 29 seconds to go, and a pair of deep passes to Moss fell incomplete. It was over—the Patriots had come oh-so-close to perfection. But they had to watch as the Giants celebrated one of the greatest upsets in NFL history.

THE BUTLER DID IT
SUPER BOWL XLIX, FEBRUARY 1, 2015

Few Super Bowls have been more entertaining—or controversial—than Super Bowl XLIX. The game featured the Patriots and the Seattle Seahawks, teams that had both started out slowly in the regular season before hitting their stride by the end.

New England held a 14–7 lead early on, but Seattle scored a touchdown with just two seconds remaining in the half to tie it. It was the start of a 17–0 Seattle run that stretched into the third quarter.

The score remained 24–14 entering the fourth quarter. The Seahawks defense was dominant, but it couldn't hold down Tom Brady forever. Brady and the Patriots struck for a touchdown with eight minutes to play, cutting the Seattle lead to three points. The Seahawks took possession of the ball, needing a long drive to put the game away. But the New England defense shut them down, forcing a punt after just three plays.

Brady and the Pats went back to work with almost seven minutes remaining. The veteran quarterback was masterful. Brady completed all eight of the passes he threw on the drive, carving up the Seattle defense and finishing off the drive with a 3-yard touchdown pass to receiver Julian Edelman. New England reclaimed the lead, 28–24.

With 2:02 left on the game clock, the Seahawks had to drive 80 yards for a touchdown—a field goal wouldn't do it. They started out fast. Quarterback Russell Wilson hit running back Marshawn Lynch for a 31-yard pass play. After Wilson converted a long third down play, the Seahawks had the ball at New England's 38-yard line.

That's when things got weird. Wilson took the snap and heaved a pass down the field. Receiver Jermaine Kearse leaped for it. But New England cornerback Malcolm Butler managed to tip the ball away an instant before it reached Kearse's hands. Both men went sprawling to the ground. The ball came down too. Somehow, it bounced off Kearse's leg, up into the air, and into the receiver's arms—all without ever touching the ground. The almost unthinkable completion left fans scratching their heads and gave the Seahawks the ball at the 5-yard line.

It seemed that almost everyone in the stadium and watching at home knew what would come next. As expected, Seattle handed the ball to Lynch, one of the league's toughest and most physical runners. No one was better equipped to hammer it in from a short distance. Lynch plowed through the Patriots defense for 4 yards.

Seattle had plenty of time. They needed just a single yard. Was there any chance New England could deny Lynch three times? It seemed unlikely.

Yet Seattle had a different idea. The Seahawks coaching staff knew that everyone was expecting another running play. So they decided to try to throw for the touchdown. The play was designed for receiver Ricardo Lockette to run a slant route over the middle, taking advantage of New England's aggressive run defense.

Only it didn't fool New England. Malcolm Butler recognized the formation. "I knew they were going to throw it," said Butler. "From preparation, I remembered the formation they were in and I knew they were doing a pick route."

As Wilson dropped back to pass, Butler sprinted toward Lockette. For a moment, the passing lane appeared clear. It was designed to be a quick-hitting play, so Wilson didn't hesitate. He zipped a pass in Lockette's direction. But Butler got there a split second before the ball did. He stepped in front of Lockette and snagged it out of the air. Interception! Just like that, the drive was over. New England let the few remaining seconds run out for one of the most shocking finishes in Super Bowl history.

Malcolm Butler *(left)* clings to the ball on the goal line. The play helped New England win Super Bowl XLIX, 28–24.

PATRIOTS MAGIC

SUPER BOWL LI, FEBRUARY 5, 2017

For two and a half quarters, Super Bowl LI had the makings of a blowout. The Atlanta Falcons had dominated the New England Patriots in every phase of the game. The Atlanta defense knocked down Tom Brady time after time, and New England's defense seemed helpless to stop quarterback Matt Ryan and the Falcons offensive attack.

Late in the third quarter, the Falcons led, 28–3. The huge lead seemed secure. No team in Super Bowl history had ever come back from more than 10 points behind. But the Patriots set out to do the unthinkable. They scored a touchdown and kicked a field goal to make the score 28–12.

Brady was hot, flinging pass after pass. With just under six minutes left in the game, he capped a New England drive with a touchdown pass to Danny Amendola. It cut the score to 28–20.

Atlanta took over and started down the field. Atlanta receiver Julio Jones made an acrobatic catch at the New England 22-yard line. The Falcons were within field goal range. Three more points for Atlanta would probably seal the win. But two plays later, New England dumped Ryan for a 12-yard sack. A holding penalty soon followed, and just like that, Atlanta was forced to punt.

Brady took over. With less than four minutes to go, he led a drive that Patriots fans will never forget. New England relentlessly pushed the ball down the field, and Atlanta couldn't stop them. The highlight of the drive came when Brady threw a pass that an Atlanta defender tipped. As the ball fluttered in the air, New England's Julian Edelman dove to catch it. He fell on top of one Atlanta defender and two others piled on top. Somehow, the ball bounced off a defender's leg and into Edelman's hands. Edelman held on, the ball just inches above the ground, for an amazing catch.

Running back James White finished the drive with a touchdown run. Then Brady hit Amendola with a pass for the two-point conversion to tie the game. Patriots fans went wild as the Falcons watched in stunned disbelief. For the first time in Super Bowl history, the game was headed to overtime.

The Patriots got the ball first in overtime. They never looked back. Brady did it again, this time with an eight-play drive that ended in another White touchdown. It was over. The greatest comeback in Super Bowl history, and one of the most incredible comebacks in all of sports, was complete. Brady had his fifth Super Bowl title—more than any other quarterback in NFL history.

James White stretches across the goal line with the ball to score the Super Bowl-winning touchdown.

3 MEMORABLE
MOMENTS

The epic matchups aren't the only reason that fans get charged up for the Super Bowl. Sometimes it's the unbelievable play, the unexpected performance, or even the unintentional comedy that gets fans going. Not every game can be a classic, but almost all Super Bowls give fans something to remember. Read on to learn about some of the most memorable moments in Super Bowl history.

GOING OUT ON TOP
SUPER BOWL II, JANUARY 14, 1968

By 1968 Vince Lombardi was already a football legend. Super Bowl II marked his final game as the head coach of the Green Bay Packers. Lombardi went out in style. The Packers were ahead 16–7 by halftime. In the fourth quarter, Green Bay defender Herb Adderley picked off a pass and returned it 60 yards for a touchdown. The Packers dominated the Oakland Raiders, 33–14, to remain the lone Super Bowl winner for a second year.

After the final seconds ticked away, Green Bay players hoisted Lombardi onto their shoulders and carried him off the field.

SWANN SONG
SUPER BOWL X, JANUARY 18, 1976

Pittsburgh Steelers wide receiver Lynn Swann wasn't expected to play in Super Bowl X against the Dallas Cowboys. The star wide receiver had suffered a concussion in the AFC Championship game, leading to a two-day hospital stay. So when Swann suited up and took the field for the Super Bowl, many assumed it would be simply as a decoy.

In 10 NFL seasons as head coach, Vince Lombardi won 96 games and lost just 34.

Swann was far more than that. He leaped and sprinted all over the field, making acrobatic catches and streaking past the Dallas defenders trying to cover him. His biggest play of the day came late in the fourth quarter. With a five-point lead, Pittsburgh faced third down on their own 36-yard line. Quarterback Terry Bradshaw took the snap. Dallas blitzed, sending a wave of pass rushers toward Bradshaw. Bradshaw managed to sidestep the blitz just long enough to heave the ball down the field.

The ball sailed through the air and into Swann's waiting arms. He caught it at the Dallas 5-yard line and trotted in for the touchdown. Bradshaw was knocked out of the game on the play, but the damage was done. Swann finished the game with 161 receiving yards and was named Super Bowl MVP.

Lynn Swann dives for the ball during Super Bowl X. He was famous for making incredible catches for the Steelers.

It was a remarkable performance under any circumstances. But for a man recently out of the hospital with a concussion, it was truly amazing. In recent decades, players and the NFL have become more aware of the long-term dangers of head injuries. In the modern game, Swann would never have been allowed to play in the Super Bowl so soon after his injury.

BOWLED OVER

SUPER BOWL XVII, JANUARY 30, 1983

Super Bowl XVII was a classic clash of styles. The Miami Dolphins used a dynamic passing attack, led by up-and-coming star quarterback Dan Marino, to blow past opponents. Meanwhile, Washington featured a powerful rushing game to pummel and wear down opposing defenses on the ground.

Miami led 17–13 with 10 minutes to play in the fourth quarter. Washington faced fourth down and one from Miami's 43-yard line. It was decision time. Washington coach Joe Gibbs could have chosen to punt and hope for a defensive stop. But instead, Gibbs decided to go for it.

Running back John Riggins took the handoff. In front of him, Washington's offensive line plowed an open path. Riggins charged through the defensive line untouched. He blasted through one attempted tackle and then sprinted all the way to the end zone. Washington never looked back, and Riggins, who totaled 166 rushing yards in the game, was named Super Bowl MVP.

THE FRIDGE PUNCHES IT IN
SUPER BOWL XX, JANUARY 26, 1986

Super Bowl XX didn't feature much drama. The Chicago Bears dominated the Patriots from start to finish. But the game featured at least one moment that fans will never forget.

The play came in the third quarter, with the game already all but out of reach for New England. The Bears led 37–3 and had driven down to the New England 1-yard line. Normally, that would have meant a handoff to legendary running back Walter Payton to stuff the ball into the end zone. But Chicago coach Mike Ditka had another idea. He put defensive lineman William "the Refrigerator" Perry in at running back. At 335 pounds (152 kilograms),

William "the Refrigerator" Perry spikes the ball after scoring a touchdown against New England. It was his fourth touchdown of the season.

the Fridge was a giant. Once he got the ball and a head of steam, there was no stopping him. Perry bowled over a defender and crashed into the end zone.

Ditka later said he regretted not giving the ball to Payton. It was the only Super Bowl the future Hall of Famer ever played in, and he never reached the end zone. Yet watching the Fridge punch it in was a highlight for many fans and a moment those who watched won't ever forget.

A STIRRING ANTHEM
SUPER BOWL XXV, JANUARY 27, 1991

Super Bowl XXV was played just 10 days after the United States became involved in the Gulf War (1990–1991) in Iraq and Kuwait. Fans watched the game with mixed feelings. On one hand, patriotism was running as high as it had in more than a generation. Yet that national pride was tempered by fear of a possible terror attack on the Super Bowl. Security for the game was ramped up like never before. The iconic Goodyear Blimp did not hover overhead in the Tampa, Florida, skies. Instead, Apache helicopters patrolled the air while SWAT teams prowled the stadium's rooftop.

The visible reminders of war contributed to a general sense of unease as superstar singer Whitney Houston stepped onto the field to sing the national anthem. Houston was one of the biggest pop stars of the day, and she'd prepared something special. Houston let loose with a rendition of "The Star-Spangled Banner" like few had ever heard. She took the upbeat anthem and slowed it down, infusing the song with soul. With an orchestra behind her, Houston captivated the crowd with every note. By the time the anthem was over—capped with a flyover of four F-16 fighter jets—the crowd was in a frenzy, and fears of an attack had seemed to melt away.

The game that followed—a one-point victory for the Giants over the Bills—was a classic nail-biter. Yet for many, Houston's stirring national anthem before the game even began was the Super Bowl XXV moment that they would never forget.

DON'T LOSE YOUR HEAD
SUPER BOWL XXVI, JANUARY 26, 1992

The Bills were back in the Super Bowl again following the 1991 season, this time to face Washington. Everything started out well for the Bills. Washington punted after just three plays on their first drive. Fans were eager to see what Buffalo's high-powered offense could do against the Washington defense.

Yet as the offense took the field, the team's biggest star and reigning NFL MVP, running back Thurman Thomas, was missing in action. Backup Kenneth Davis lined up in his place. Quarterback Jim Kelly took the snap for Buffalo's first offensive play of the game and handed off to Davis, who gained just a single yard.

Meanwhile, confusion reigned on the Buffalo sideline. Thomas couldn't find his helmet. The superstar had a routine of leaving his helmet in the same place before every game. But when he'd returned from the coin toss on the field, the helmet was nowhere to be found. He, along with Buffalo's equipment staff, searched frantically for it. Meanwhile, the game carried on. On second down, Kelly scrambled for a 4-yard gain.

"You really can't explain it," Thomas later said. "When I think back on it, I should have known something was going to happen bad. It was a culmination of a nightmare."

Panic on the sideline grew by the moment, until the helmet was finally found on the end of the bench (another Buffalo player had likely picked it up, mistaking it for his own). Thomas made it out for the third play of the game, though Buffalo was still forced to punt. It was a disastrous beginning to the game, and the Bills never recovered. Thomas managed just 13 yards rushing on 10 carries. With so little production out of the league MVP, the Bills never stood a chance. Washington went on to a comfortable 37–24 victory.

NOT SO FAST

Not much went right for the Bills in Super Bowl XXVII. With about five minutes remaining in the fourth quarter, they trailed the Cowboys, 52–17. Bills backup quarterback Frank Reich dropped back to pass but was blasted by Dallas defender Jim Jeffcoat. The ball popped loose and was scooped up by one of the biggest players on the field, 290-pound (132 kg) defensive lineman Leon Lett.

Lett had nothing but 65 yards of open field in front of him. A touchdown would give Dallas the all-time Super Bowl scoring record. Lett, seeing no Buffalo players to stand in his way, held the ball out at arm's length, celebrating as he ran.

Bills receiver Don Beebe never gave up on the play, however. Beebe streaked down the field at full speed. He caught the showboating Lett—who was oblivious to Beebe's pursuit—just before

Leon Lett rumbles toward the end zone as Don Beebe sneaks up behind him to swat the ball away at the last second. The play didn't have an impact on the final score, but it may have been Super Bowl XXVII's most memorable moment.

the goal line. Beebe reached in and swatted the ball out of Lett's hand. It bounced through the end zone for a touchback, denying Dallas the scoring record.

ELWAY'S HELICOPTER
SUPER BOWL XXXII, JANUARY 25, 1998

At the age of 37, Denver Broncos quarterback John Elway knew that he wouldn't have many more chances to win a Super Bowl. So he was determined to leave it all on the field as the Broncos faced the heavily favored Packers in Super Bowl XXXII.

After Denver had jumped out to an early 17–7 lead, the Packers charged back, tying the game. Denver needed a big play to reverse the momentum. Elway provided one—though not in the way that anyone would have guessed.

Facing third down on the Green Bay 12-yard line, Elway took the snap. He scanned the field, but Green Bay defenders blanketed all of his receivers. Elway could have thrown the ball away and settled for a field goal attempt. But instead, he tucked it under his arm to run. The 37-year-old charged, surprising many Green Bay defenders, who quickly converged on the quarterback.

Elway barreled downfield, knowing that it was all for nothing if he didn't reach the first-down marker. So when he saw Green Bay safety LeRoy Butler near the 6-yard line—right at the marker—Elway didn't slide or shy away from what he knew would be a brutal hit. Instead, he launched himself into the air.

Butler unloaded, clipping Elway mid-dive. The impact sent Elway spinning in the air like the blades of a helicopter. As the quarterback came down, another Packer defender came in with a second bone-rattling hit.

Elway's high-impact run had gained 8 yards—enough for a first down. The Broncos went on to score a touchdown and win the game. A year later, they repeated as champs, sending Elway into retirement as a two-time Super Bowl winner.

ANYTHING YOU CAN DO, I CAN DO BETTER
SUPER BOWL XXXV, JANUARY 28, 2001

The closing moments of the third quarter in Super Bowl XXXV were wild, to say the least. The Baltimore Ravens took a 17–0 lead when defensive back Duane Starks picked off a pass from the New York Giants quarterback Kerry Collins and returned it for a touchdown.

Any chance of winning seemed to be slipping away from the Giants. That is until Ron Dixon fielded the ensuing kickoff. Dixon, a dynamic return man, sliced through Baltimore's coverage team, going 97 yards for a touchdown. In a game where New York's offense had sputtered against the dominating Ravens' defense, it was a rare glimmer of hope for Giants fans.

With no one in front of him, Baltimore's Jermaine Lewis looks over his shoulder for defenders as he scampers to the end zone.

The good feeling didn't last long, however. That's because just one play later, Baltimore return man Jermaine Lewis returned the favor. Lewis fielded the ball at his own 16-yard line and followed a wall of blockers toward the right sideline. With one final burst of speed, Lewis outpaced the final defender and took it to the end zone. Just like that, the Giants' faint spark of hope was extinguished.

GAME WINNER

SUPER BOWL XXXVI, FEBRUARY 3, 2002

Super Bowl XXXVI was filled with memorable moments. They started even before the opening kickoff was in the air. The New England Patriots, bucking pregame tradition, ran onto the field as a team, rather than as individuals. It was a gesture of unity that fans appreciated. The United States was only months removed from the September 11, 2001, terror attacks in New York City and near Washington, DC. The game was marked by a stirring second-half comeback by the St. Louis Rams. The Rams erased a 14-point deficit before first-year starting quarterback Tom Brady led the Patriots down the field on the game's final drive.

Adam Vinatieri gets the party started before his Super Bowl-winning kick even hits the ground.

With time running out and the score tied at 17, Brady marched the Patriots into Rams territory. Just seven seconds remained when he spiked the ball at the Rams' 30-yard line to stop the clock and set up a 48-yard field goal attempt. Fans roared in the stands as kicker Adam Vinatieri booted the game-winner through the goalposts to give New England the thrilling victory.

Vinatieri's kick marked the beginning of one of the NFL's greatest dynasties. Over the next decade and a half, Brady and the Patriots would reach the Super Bowl six times, winning four of them.

QUICK STRIKE

SUPER BOWL XLI, FEBRUARY 4, 2007

Super Bowl XLI started out with a bang. The crowd roared in anticipation as Adam Vinatieri, now with the Indianapolis Colts, prepared to boot the opening kickoff toward return specialist Devin Hester. Hester—a rookie—had burned opponents all season with his electrifying returns, including an NFL record six returns for touchdowns. Hester was such a threat that many experts had suggested that Indianapolis use a tactic called a squib kick—a short kick designed to prevent big returns. But the Colts weren't interested in such a strategy. They were confident they could contain Hester. So Vinatieri kicked it deep.

It was one of the few mistakes the Colts would make all game. Hester fielded the kick at the 8-yard line, near the left sideline. As the Colts coverage team crashed through Chicago blockers, Hester hesitated a moment, then darted toward the middle of the field. Hester cut left, then right again, before finding open space. He blazed down the field, veering toward the right sideline as the Colts desperately pursued. With Hester's tremendous speed, it was a pointless pursuit.

Chicago's Devin Hester sidesteps the outstretched arm of Adam Vinatieri on his way to a 92-yard touchdown return.

He cruised into the end zone to give the Bears a lead, just 14 seconds into the game. It remains the only time the Super Bowl's opening kickoff has been returned for a touchdown.

Bears fans were in a frenzy. But those good feelings didn't last long. Indianapolis had learned their lesson and never kicked deep again. With Hester neutralized, the Bears couldn't muster nearly enough offense to keep up with the high-powered Colts. Indy cruised to a 29–17 victory, and by game's end, Hester's big return seemed like a distant memory.

ACCIDENTAL TOUCHDOWN
SUPER BOWL XLVI, FEBRUARY 2012

One of the funniest plays in Super Bowl history came in Super Bowl XLVI, when New York Giants running back Ahmad Bradshaw scored a touchdown . . . by accident.

With just over a minute to play in the fourth quarter, the Giants trailed the New England Patriots, 17–15. The Giants were on the move, driving toward a winning score. With the ball on the New England 6-yard line, quarterback Eli Manning handed the ball to Ahmad Bradshaw. Bradshaw and the Giants needed to score, but they also wanted to kill time, making sure not to leave the Patriots a chance to get the ball back. Meanwhile, Patriots defenders were planning to let Bradshaw score the touchdown, knowing that giving the ball back to Tom Brady and the New England offense with time on the game clock was their only real shot.

"I took the handoff and said [to myself], 'Don't score, don't score,'" Bradshaw explained. But as he charged through the intentionally soft defense, Bradshaw couldn't manage to follow his own advice. Too late, he pulled up, trying to fall down onto his bottom at the 1-yard line. His momentum, however, carried him over the goal line and into the end zone for one of the least graceful and least wanted Super Bowl touchdowns of all time.

It all worked out in the end for the Giants. The Patriots responded to Bradshaw's score by driving to midfield. But Brady's final desperate pass was deflected, giving the Giants the victory and allowing Bradshaw to breathe easy.

LIGHTS OUT

SUPER BOWL XLVII, FEBRUARY 3, 2013

Ahmad Bradshaw flops backward into the end zone to give the Giants the lead.

Super Bowl XLVII in New Orleans, Louisiana, was a clash of brothers at head coach. Jim Harbaugh coached the 49ers, while John Harbaugh manned the sidelines for the Baltimore Ravens. John Harbaugh and the Ravens took control of the "Harbaugh Bowl" early, building a 21–6 halftime lead. Then, to start the second half, Baltimore's Jacoby Jones returned the opening kickoff 108 yards to extend the lead to 28–6.

It may have seemed as if the lights were about to go out on San Francisco's season. And then something unthinkable happened. Not long after the 49ers took possession of the ball, the lights in the Superdome flickered and died.

Emergency generators quickly kicked in, powering the stadium's emergency lighting. The fans and media were confused. Players wandered around the dimly lit field, staring up in wonder. Meanwhile, maintenance crews and NFL officials scrambled to figure out what had happened and how to fix it.

Ravens players weren't sure what to do when the stadium lights cut out during the third quarter of Super Bowl XLVII.

After a delay of 34 minutes, the problem—faulty electrical equipment within the stadium—was fixed. The lights came back on to the roar of the crowd. The game was ready to resume.

It was as if someone had flicked a switch on the 49ers as well. They'd been dominated all game. But once the power came back on, quarterback Colin Kaepernick led a furious charge to get San Francisco back in the game. With about 10 minutes left in the fourth quarter, Kaepernick threw a touchdown pass that cut the Ravens' lead to 31–29. The 49ers went for a two-point conversion to tie the game, but Kaepernick's pass fell incomplete.

Baltimore responded with a field goal, but the 49ers had one last shot. Kaepernick marched the team down the field. Everyone in the stadium was in a frenzy as the 49ers reached Baltimore's 7-yard line. But they couldn't finish it off. Baltimore's defense stepped up, stopping the 49ers there and sealing the victory.

4 BEYOND TOUCHDOWNS AND TACKLES:
THE ACTION OFF THE FIELD

For die-hard football fans, the action on the field is what the Super Bowl is all about. But the modern Super Bowl has grown into an event that stretches far beyond touchdowns and tackles. It has become a cultural event and a virtual national holiday. The festivities stretch over more than a week, including some of the stranger traditions in all of sports.

PREPARING FOR THE BIG DAY

The preparation for a Super Bowl starts months and even years before it takes place. Host cities must plan for the swarms of visitors. That can include upgrading public transportation and roads, building additional lodging, and upgrading the stadium itself.

The preparation really kicks into high gear once the two teams are set. The teams usually arrive in the host city about a week before the game. While players practice, fans and media enjoy a wide range of events. Fans flock to the NFL Experience, a theme park where they play games, collect autographs, and take

Fans of all ages can have a blast at NFL Experience events.

photos. In the days leading up to the big game, fans take in concerts, shopping, and sample local food.

Meanwhile, the media blitz begins as soon as the two teams are decided. Reporters from around the country and the world travel to the Super Bowl. One of the most unusual aspects of Super Bowl week is the infamous media day. Players field a wide array of questions, including the strange and often nonsensical, while fans look on. Some players seem to revel in the attention and enjoy the antics. Others appear annoyed at the whole process.

By Super Bowl Sunday, the media coverage is at a fever pitch. Network television pregame coverage starts in the morning—hours before the game. Every angle, story, and statistic is told and retold as fans gear up for kickoff.

COUNTDOWN TO KICKOFF

On the afternoon of game day, the stadium begins to fill. Often popular musicians or marching bands perform at the stadium. The players dress and prepare in their locker rooms. When the time comes, they burst out onto the field to thunderous applause.

As kickoff approaches, the formal television coverage begins. The stadium grows quiet as a singer—usually a pop or country star—comes out to sing the national anthem, often along with "America the Beautiful." It's a show of patriotism, with huge, flapping US flags, flanks of US military personnel, and even flyovers of military jets.

Next comes the coin toss. Several current players, along with honorary team captains (usually legends from each team's past), gather at midfield. All the pomp and circumstance don't add up to a whole lot, though. Teams that win the toss usually defer anyway, leaving the choice to their opponent.

Finally, it's time for the main event. The field is cleared, and the kickoff and return teams take the field as the roar from the stands reaches a fever pitch. The kicker places the ball on the tee and waits for the referee's signal to begin. The biggest game in the world is about to begin.

THE HALFTIME SHOW

The Super Bowl Halftime Show wasn't always the extravaganza it is today. At first, halftime was an afterthought, often featuring marching bands from local universities to entertain the fans while the players nursed their bruises. The first Super Bowl halftime show featured trumpeter Al Hirt. An image of Hirt shows him playing to mostly empty stands (fans were likely getting food or on restroom breaks).

Popular music stars started performing at halftime in the early 1970s. But still, they were there mainly to fill the time while players and coaches regrouped in their locker rooms. By the 1980s, the show had grown into an event more geared for television, yet the performances themselves remained largely forgettable tributes to music eras of the past. The Super Bowl Halftime Show made little effort to be a memorable part of the game.

That began to change in 1991, when pop group New Kids on the Block took the stage. For the first time, the show featured a modern act performing current hits. Two years later, Michael Jackson almost single-handedly elevated the Halftime Show from bathroom-break material to must-see television. By the 2000s, the Halftime Show was reserved for only the biggest of acts—from U2 to Justin Timberlake to Beyoncé. Among the most famous was the 2007 show, which featured an electric performance from Prince amid pouring rain.

Fans took part in the fun at the 2016 Super Bowl Halftime Show.

The Denver Broncos celebrate after winning Super Bowl 50 at Levi's Stadium on February 7, 2016.

WRAPPING UP

After the final seconds have ticked off the clock and a champion is crowned, the postgame festivities begin. The winning players, coaches, staff, and their families flood the field, flanked by hoards of reporters. Music blares. Confetti flitters down onto the victors.

Workers quickly wheel a stage out onto the field for the trophy presentation. The team owner, coaches, and a handful of players stand with the NFL commissioner and a TV broadcast team to receive the Vince Lombardi Trophy as Super Bowl champions.

Next comes the announcement of the game's MVP. A panel of reporters, with the help of an online fan vote, picks the player who had the biggest impact on the game. This player almost invariably comes from the winning team (about half of the time, it's the winning quarterback). Only once, in 1971, has a member of the losing team walked away with the honor.

As the fans filter out of the stadium and the celebrations begin to die out, the spectacle known as Super Bowl Week comes to a close. Players, coaches, sportswriters, and fans may go on analyzing every play and every decision for months or even years. But already, the host city of next year's game is on the clock—just 51 more weeks until the Super Bowl excitement starts all over again.

THE VINCE LOMBARDI TROPHY

The Super Bowl winners are presented with the Vince Lombardi Trophy (*below*), named for former NFL coach Vince Lombardi, who coached the Packers to victory in each of the first two Super Bowls.

The sterling silver trophy depicts a football set in a kicking position. The words "Vince Lombardi Trophy" are engraved in the silver, along with the roman numeral of that year's Super Bowl. After the champion is crowned, the final score, date, and location of the game are added. Each member of the winning team also receives a Super Bowl ring.

There's a financial reward for the players as well, though it generally pales in comparison to their salaries. For Super Bowl 50, members of the winning Denver Broncos each earned $102,000. The players on the losing Carolina Panthers got $51,000 each.

5 THE FUTURE
OF THE SUPER BOWL

The NFL has come a long way from its inaugural season, and nothing better illustrates that than its biggest game. The Super Bowl has grown from a small-time clash between league champions into the biggest annual sporting event in the world.

In North America, the popularity of the NFL is unrivaled among sports leagues. But many experts and league officials believe that the NFL won't be content to remain a strictly US affair. For decades, the league has worked to pave the way toward an international presence, starting with Europe. In 1991 it started the World League of American Football (WLAF) to build fan interest in Europe. Later called the NFL Europe League, it served mainly as a training ground for players who were unable to make the cut for NFL rosters. The league folded after the 2007 season.

In 2007 the NFL started its International Series, which consists of regular-season NFL games held outside the United States. The early focus of the series was on London, England. In 2016 it expanded to Mexico City, Mexico, as well. Many experts believe that the league's success in London will eventually land a team there, either a new team or a franchise that wishes to move from its current city. That would make the NFL a truly worldwide affair and could pave the way for international NFL divisions—and the possibility of a Super Bowl being hosted outside of the United States.

The NFL Europe League had the hard hits and great catches football fans expect, but the league didn't catch on.

Security has also become a growing concern. After the terror attacks of September 11, 2001, security at the Super Bowl has been beefed up. It involves the National Guard, the Federal Bureau of Investigation (FBI), and other law enforcement agencies. Metal detectors scan fans for weapons. Bomb-sniffing dogs search for threats, while military aircraft secure the skies around the stadium. Increasing security is a trend that's likely to grow in the future as law enforcement uses the latest technology to keep the game safe.

Meanwhile, a different kind of dark cloud hangs over the league, threatening to fundamentally change the game as fans know it. In recent decades, medical data has shown in great detail the dangers of concussions and other brain injuries that football players face. Brain injuries can cause memory and thinking problems, headaches and blurry vision, and a host of other symptoms. Pro football has always been a hard-hitting, violent game. As players get larger and faster, the hits get bigger and more destructive. A 2016 study showed that 40 percent of retired NFL players showed some sign of brain injury.

The league has already begun to respond. It started with improved protective gear, including state-of-the-art helmets designed to soften blows to the head. Rules already prohibit certain kinds of hits, such as helmet-to-helmet hits on quarterbacks and against defenseless players, which are known to cause concussions. And as data—and lawsuits—continue to pile up, future rule changes will further improve player safety. But some fans wonder where it ends. By its nature, football is a

When two NFL players meet, they can create a fearsome collision. The league often changes rules in an attempt to make the game safer.

Fans celebrate the Denver Broncos 24–10 victory over the Carolina Panthers at Super Bowl 50 at Levi's Stadium.

violent sport. Tackles, blocks, and other hard hits are woven into the very fabric of the game. How far can the rule changes go before the game itself stops resembling the game that fans love? Where will the NFL and its players draw the line? And what will the play on the field look like in Super Bowls 60, 75, or 100?

One thing is certain. Fans can't seem to get enough of the NFL. As they keep tabs on their favorite teams from the off-season through the playoffs, fan enthusiasm for the NFL's grand showcase, the Super Bowl, keeps growing and growing.

RECORD BOOK

The Super Bowl has seen its share of amazing performances. Check out some of the game's most astonishing records.

TEAM RECORDS

MOST SUPER BOWL APPEARANCES

New England Patriots	9
Dallas Cowboys	8
Denver Broncos	8
Pittsburgh Steelers	8

MOST SUPER BOWL VICTORIES

Pittsburgh Steelers	6
Dallas Cowboys	5
New England Patriots	5
San Francisco 49ers	5

MOST POINTS SCORED IN A SUPER BOWL

San Francisco 49ers, Super Bowl XXIV	55
Dallas Cowboys, Super Bowl XXVII	52
San Francisco 49ers, Super Bowl XXIX	49

FEWEST POINTS SCORED AGAINST A DEFENSE IN A SUPER BOWL

Dallas Cowboys, Super Bowl VI	3
Pittsburgh Steelers, Super Bowl IX	6
Five teams tied	7

Individual Records

Most Passing Yards in a Super Bowl

Tom Brady, New England Patriots, LI	466
Kurt Warner, St. Louis Rams, XXXIV	414
Kurt Warner, Arizona Cardinals, XLIII	377

Most Receiving Yards in a Super Bowl

Jerry Rice, San Francisco 49ers, XXIII	215
Ricky Sanders, Washington Redskins, XXII	193
Isaac Bruce, St. Louis Rams, XXXIV	162

Most Rushing Yards in a Super Bowl

Timmy Smith, Washington Redskins, XXII	204
Marcus Allen, Los Angeles Raiders, XVIII	191
John Riggins, Washington Redskins, XVII	166

Most Sacks in a Super Bowl

Darnell Dockett, Arizona Cardinals, XLIII	3
Kony Ealy, Carolina Panthers, SB50	3
Grady Jarrett, Atlanta Falcons, LI	3
Reggie White, Green Bay Packers, XXXI	3

Most Super Bowl MVP Awards

Tom Brady	4
Joe Montana	3
Terry Bradshaw	2
Eli Manning	2
Bart Starr	2

SOURCE NOTES

21   Les Carpenter, "Nothing Like Namath's Guarantee," *Washington Post*, January 30, 2007, http://www
.washingtonpost.com/wp-dyn/content/article/2007/01/29/AR2007012901789.html.

22–23   Larry Fox, "Super Bowl XIII: Steelers First 3-Time Winner in Super Thriller, 35–31," *New York Daily
News*, December 30, 2013, http://www.nydailynews.com/sports/football/super-bowl-xiii-steelers-3-time
-winner-super-thriller-35-31-article-1.1559716.

25   John Shea, "Super Bowl XXIII: Montana in His Cool Best in Drive for the Ages," *San Francisco Chronicle*,
last modified January 25, 2016, http://www.sfgate.com/49ers/article/Super-Bowl-XXIII-Montana-at-his
-cool-best-in-6779819.php.

31   Peter King, "The Super Bowl That Took Everyone's Breath Away," *Sports Illustrated*, February 2, 2015,
http://mmqb.si.com/2015/02/02/super-bowl-49-patriots-defeat-seahawks.

39   Paul Attner, "The Case of the Disappearing Helmet: Why in Hell Couldn't It Have Been Where Thurman
Thomas Left It? He Put It Down near the Bench Like He Always Does, Then It Disappeared. Incident
in 37–24 loss in Super Bowl XXVI Continues to Haunt Bills' Back," *Los Angeles Times*, October 4, 1992,
http://articles.latimes.com/1992-10-04/sports/sp-1056_1_super-bowl-xxvi.

45   Robert Klemko, "Bradshaw Falls into End Zone, Super Bowl Lore," *USA Today*, February 6, 2012, http://
usatoday30.usatoday.com/SPORTS/usaedition/2012-02-06-SB-game-side-0206_ST_U.htm.

GLOSSARY

blitz: a play in which a defense uses players to rush the quarterback who do not normally do so

charter member: an original, or founding, member of an organization

concussion: a brain injury that may cause memory loss, dizziness, and other symptoms

controversial: disputed or giving rise to public disagreement

dynasty: a prolonged period of dominance by a team or athlete

formation: the way a team lines up before a play

franchise: a team and the organization around it, including the owner, ticket sellers, and others

lateral: a throw that travels backwards or sideways from the line of scrimmage

monopoly: exclusive control over a product or service

onside kick: an intentionally short kick that the kicking team can try to recover

play-action pass: a play disguised to look like a running play, complete with a fake handoff

sack: tackle a quarterback behind the line of scrimmage for a loss of yards

wild card: a team that qualifies for the playoffs despite not winning its division

FURTHER READING

Doeden, Matt. *The College Football Championship: The Fight for the Top Spot*. Minneapolis: Millbrook Press, 2016.

Ellenport, Craig. *The Super Bowl: More Than a Game*. Broomall, PA: Mason Crest, 2017.

Fischer, David. *The Super Bowl: The First Fifty Years of America's Greatest Game*. New York: Sports Publishing, 2015.

Myers, Gary. *Brady vs Manning: The Untold Story of the Rivalry That Transformed the NFL*. New York: Crown Archetype, 2015.

NFL
http://www.nfl.com

Pro Football Hall of Fame
http://www.profootballhof.com

Pro Football Reference
http://www.pro-football-reference.com

Schultz, Randy. *Legends of the Buffalo Bills: Marv Levy, Bruce Smith, Thurman Thomas, and other Bills Stars*. New York: Sports Publishing, 2015.

Sports Illustrated editors. *Super Bowl Gold: 50 Years of the Big Game*. New York: Sports Illustrated Books, 2015.

Super Bowl History
https://www.nfl.com/super-bowl/history

INDEX

ABOUT THE AUTHOR

Matt Doeden began his career as a sportswriter. Since then he's spent more than a decade writing and editing more than 100 children's nonfiction books. His books *The Negro Leagues: Celebrating Baseball's Unsung Heroes, The World Series: Baseball's Biggest Stage, Sandy Koufax,* and *Tom Brady: Unlikely Champion* were Junior Library Guild selections. Doeden lives in Minnesota with his wife and two children.

PHOTO ACKNOWLEDGMENTS